USBORNE HOTSHOTS
DRAWING
CARTOONS

SCHOLASTIC INC.

New York   Toronto   London   Auckland   Sydney

USBORNE HOTSHOTS
DRAWING CARTOONS

Edited by Alastair Smith
Designed by Karen Tomlins

Illustrated by Terry Bave and Graham Round

Photographs by Howard Allman

Series editor: Judy Tatchell
Series designer: Ruth Russell

CONTENTS

First faces

The instructions on these two pages show you an easy way to draw cartoon faces.

Draw a circle. Do two pencil lines crossing it (1). Put the nose where the lines cross. The ears are level with the nose, and the eyes go above it (2).

When you have drawn the features, erase the pencil lines crossing the face (3). Complete the face with bright pencils or felt tips (4).

Faces to copy

In a cartoon, you can exaggerate things such as the shape and size of the nose or mouth, to create different expressions.

Looking around

As a face looks to one side, the line going down the face curves to that side.

As the face turns farther around, this line also moves farther around.

This shows a face seen from the front.

The face starts to look to one side.

The face turns even farther around.

A side view is called a profile.

1.

2.

Tilting heads

To make a face look up or down (1, 2 and 3) curve the line across the face up or down. To make the face look up and to one side (4) curve both lines that cross the face.

3.

4.

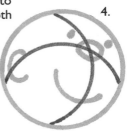

Cartoon people

You can add bodies to cartoon heads by drawing sticks for the trunk and limbs and filling the body out around them. Use a pencil for the sticks so you can erase them later.

Trunk stick

Pelvis stick

Stick figures

Make the trunk slightly longer than the head. The legs should be slightly longer than the trunk and the arms. Keep the pelvis short or the figure will end up bottom-heavy.

Adding clothes

Here are some suggestions for clothes. Try the sweatshirt with jeans or a skirt. You could also try a jacket or a dress.

To dress the stick figure, draw the clothes around it, starting at the neck and working down. When you add hair, erase a little of the head circle if the hair falls forward over it.

Hands and shoes

Cartoon hands and shoes, like cartoon heads, are larger than on a real person. Try these shapes.

Finishing off

When you have finished the outline of the figure, go over it with a fine felt-tip pen. When it is dry you can erase the stick figure and decorate the character's clothes.

Try to keep the outline smooth.

Shiny white patches on toes of shoes.

When you decorate shoes, leave a small, white patch on the toes to make them look shiny. A person with bare legs needs to have lines for the legs drawn in before you can add the shoes.

You can put socks on bare legs.

7

Making faces

You can make cartoon people come to life by giving them different expressions. To do this, you may only need to add or change a few lines. Try copying the expressions on these two pages.

Smug. Sideways grin and half-closed eyes.

Sickly. Face has a greenish tinge. Tongue hangs out.

Worried. Forehead is frowning and mouth droops.

Winking. Mouth tilts up on side where eye is closed.

Thoughtful. Eyes look up and sideways.

Frightened. Face is pale and bluish. Hair stands on end. Eyes are wide open.

Yawning. Nose squashes up to closed eyes. Mouth is wide, showing teeth.

Sly. Eyes look sideways and mouth is pursed.

Angry. Use strong lines for the mouth and eyebrows.

Sad. The mouth and eyebrows droop.

Cartoons growing up

As people grow older, their bodies change shape.
So does the way they stand, sit and move.

Babies

A baby is rounded with a large
head and short limbs. The
head is about one third
the length of the body.

The features are all in
the lower half
of the face.

*Short,
chubby
limbs.*

*Not much
hair.*

*High,
round
forehead.*

*Eyes half
way down
face.*

Children

Children's heads are still large in proportion to
their bodies. There is more space between the
chin and mouth than on a baby.

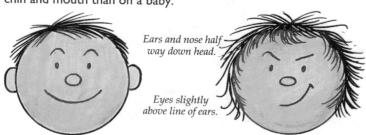

*Ears and nose half
way down head.*

*Eyes slightly
above line of ears.*

Men and women

A woman's face and body are usually rounder than a man's. Putting her eyes wider apart also makes her face look rounder.

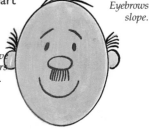

Eyebrows slope.

Eyes above line of ears and nose.

Round eyebrows give a soft shape.

A man's face is more oval than round. Make the nose bigger than on a woman or child.

An adult's head is just under a quarter of the length of the body.

Old people tend to be bent over. Their heads are placed farther forward.

Old people

Old people are usually smaller than younger adults. Their faces are round, like babies' faces. They have small eyes and sloping eyebrows.

Hair grows farther back on head.

Ears low down on the side of the head.

Different views

It is useful to be able to draw people from the side and back as well as from the front. The figures on the right show the basic shapes. You could sketch these first to get the proportions. Then draw the outline of the person around them and finish as shown on the left.

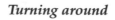

Turning around

As a person begins to turn around, the body gets narrower.

Right arm overlaps body.

Right leg overlaps left.

Side view

From the side, the body is at its narrowest. You can see the shape of the nose and back of one hand.

Right arm is at back of body shape.

Left leg just visible behind right.

Back view

From the back, the body parts are the same sizes and shapes as from the front.

The backs of the heels will be visible.

12

More positions to draw

Here are lots of cartoon people, in all
sorts of positions. Copying them will
help you to draw people in other
positions, too.

*Sketch the figures
roughly before
adding details.*

*Sketch the figure
before starting
the bicycle.*

*A piggy back is
tricky to draw
because the limbs
are all mixed up.*

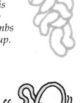

*Draw the lasso last,
after you have finished
sketching the figure.*

13

Moving pictures

Here are a few tricks that you can use to make your action pictures of people look more convincing. It might help to start by drawing a stick figure.

Walking and running

A walking person leans forward slightly. There is always one foot on the ground. A running person leans forward more. The elbows bend and move back and forth.

The right arm is in front when the left leg is forward.

Draw the figure above ground level to show he is on the move.

Blobs of sweat flying off head.

The faster somebody runs, the more the body leans forward and the farther the arms stretch.

Add a few curved lines to show fast movement.

Action pictures

These pictures all show movement. Try them for yourself, starting with a sketch of the basic stick figure.

Curved lines show the swing of the racket.

These lines show the path of the ball.

The body twists toward the foot that is kicking.

Lines indicate the speed and direction of the movement.

Falling over

These pictures show a stick person running downstairs and tripping. You could copy the stick shapes and then fill in the body shapes around the stick figures.

More movement

By exaggerating certain things you can give an impression of lots of speed or effort.

To give a sense of speed, draw hair and items of clothing, such as a scarf, streaming out behind.

Adding words on a picture can give extra impact. Make the letters big and bold. You could do them in red or yellow, to make them eye-catching.

Clouds of dust

The person opposite is running to catch a bus. You can add a word like ZOOM or WHIZZ, with an exclamation mark.

The figures below are running away. They are small, as if they are in the distance. The dust clouds also get smaller as they get farther away.

ZIP!

A curved line for the ground gives a feeling of space and distance covered.

Beads of perspiration.

Clenched fists.

You can add movement lines around the letters.

Legs spinning.

ZOOM!

Freeze frame

You can draw pictures that look frozen in the middle of exciting action, as if you were freezing a video during a film.

Ski pole flying through the air.

Wide mouth and eyes and spinning head make him look confused.

17

Scenery and backgrounds

Scenery can help when you want a picture to have an
impression of distance, or depth. Drawing pictures
with depth is called drawing in perspective.

Tricks of perspective

The farther away something is,
the smaller it looks. The
woman in this picture is drawn
smaller than the burglar to
make her look farther away.

Draw the woman farther up
the page than the burglar.
Otherwise she might just look
like a tiny person, as shown in
the picture above.

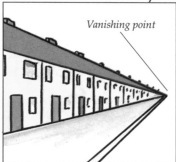

Vanishing point

Parallel lines appear to get
closer the farther away they
are. They seem to meet at a
point on the horizon. This is
called the vanishing point.

A high vanishing point makes it
appear as if you are looking
down on the picture. What do
you think happens if you draw
a low vanishing point?

A picture in perspective

Here is a picture in perspective. The woman is drawn smaller and farther up than the burglar to make her look farther away.

If the vanishing point falls outside your picture area, try sketching it in pencil. This helps to get the lines in perspective.

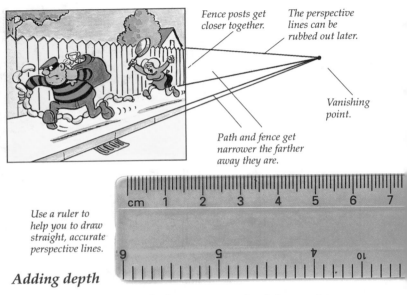

Fence posts get closer together.

The perspective lines can be rubbed out later.

Vanishing point.

Path and fence get narrower the farther away they are.

Use a ruler to help you to draw straight, accurate perspective lines.

Adding depth

Here are more ways in which you can get depth into a picture.

Lines of hills show that scene goes back for miles.

Scenery is paler and less distinct in the distance.

Man is large because he is nearest to you.

Strip cartoons

Strip cartoons are stories told using a
sequence of pictures. It is tricky to make
characters look the same in each picture frame, so
give them features that you find easy to draw.

How to start

Think of a theme first
and make up a joke
around it. Keep the idea
simple and direct.

Divide the joke into three or four stages. You can vary the frame
sizes, and mix close-ups with larger scenes, to make it interesting.

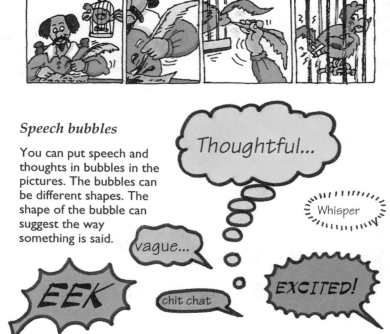

Speech bubbles

You can put speech and
thoughts in bubbles in the
pictures. The bubbles can
be different shapes. The
shape of the bubble can
suggest the way
something is said.

The tips here will help you to create tidy lettering inside speech bubbles.

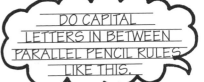

DO CAPITAL LETTERS IN BETWEEN PARALLEL PENCIL RULES LIKE THIS.

MAKE EACH LINE ROUGHLY THE SAME LENGTH. DRAW A VERTICAL RULE. PUT THE SAME NUMBER OF LETTERS EITHER SIDE OF THE RULE ON EACH LINE.

A finished strip

Use bright felt-tips to make characters stand out, and paler shades for the background. Sound effects make the strip more fun and bring it to life.

Put speech bubbles over sky, or other undetailed areas. Position them from left to right down the frame, so that people read them in the right order.

Special effects

Special effects can make cartoons look exciting. Here are some ideas for how to add drama and atmosphere to your pictures.

Shadows and silhouettes

Using different lighting effects for night pictures can make them look scary.

These silhouettes are made by people sitting in front of a source of light.

A lightning flash behind a castle turns it into a spooky silhouette.

Huge shadows on a wall look threatening.

Sound effects

You can add sound effects by using words and shapes which suggest the sound. The most common ones are explosions but there are lots of others you can use.

This jagged speech bubble suggests a sudden shout and helps to show the man's shock.

Two finished strips

These strip cartoons use some of the special effects described on these pages.

Cartoon animals

You can draw cartoon animals in a similar way to cartoon people, by using simple shapes and lines and adding features. You can use their natural characteristics, such as claws, tails and ears, to give them personality.

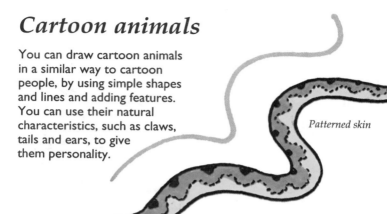

Patterned skin

Forked tongue

Snake

Draw a wriggly shape. Then fill out the body and add a rounded head.

Elephant

Start by drawing two circles, one inside the other. Then add ears and a trunk.

Flapping ears

Curly, wrinkly trunk

Pig

Start with three circles. The middle one is the snout.

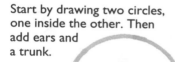

Back view

Curly tail

Dog

A dog's head is slightly pointed at the top.

Floppy ears

Wagging tail

Cat

A cat has a rounder head than a dog.

Egg-shaped body

Add face, ears and sticks for arms and legs.

Mouse

Start with two circles, one slightly larger than the other.

Big ears

Big teeth

Long tail

Bird

A bird has an egg-shaped body with a small, round head.

Long thin legs

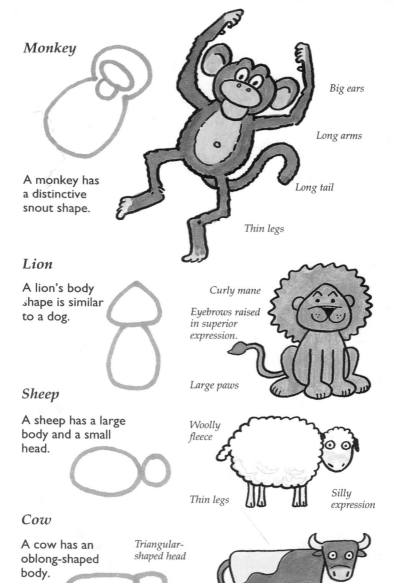

Monkey

A monkey has a distinctive snout shape.

Big ears

Long arms

Long tail

Thin legs

Lion

A lion's body shape is similar to a dog.

Curly mane

Eyebrows raised in superior expression.

Large paws

Sheep

A sheep has a large body and a small head.

Woolly fleece

Thin legs

Silly expression

Cow

A cow has an oblong-shaped body.

Triangular-shaped head

Horns and ears

Udder

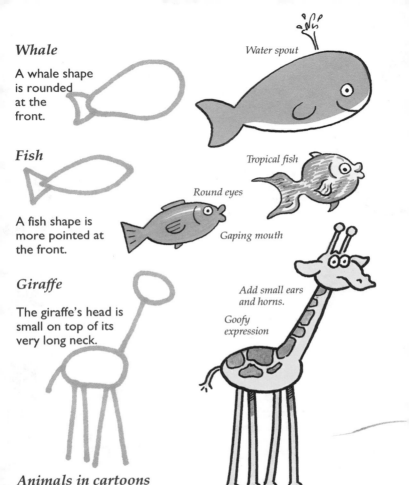

Whale

A whale shape is rounded at the front.

Water spout

Fish

A fish shape is more pointed at the front.

Tropical fish

Round eyes

Gaping mouth

Giraffe

The giraffe's head is small on top of its very long neck.

Add small ears and horns.

Goofy expression

Animals in cartoons

Cartoons may look violent but no real harm is done. This cartoon might help you think up a few of your own animal cartoons.

Drawing materials

Here is a guide to some equipment that you might find useful for drawing cartoons. All of these are available at art materials shops and you can buy some at an ordinary stationers.

Pencils

Pencils are marked from 9H to 7B, depending on how hard (H) or soft (B for black) they are. The most useful range is between about 2H and 2B.

A medium hard (2H) pencil will mark paper easily, but will not smudge.

Technical drawing pens

A technical drawing pen with a fine point gives precise, inked outlines. This sort of pen is also useful for doing comic strip lettering.

Technical drawing pens are expensive but give tidy results.

Felt-tips

A very fine felt-tip is a cheaper alternative to a technical pen.

Felt-tips give strong tones which are good for cartoons. They come with different types of tips for different purposes.

A fine felt-tip is good for detail.

A broad felt-tip is ideal for filling in large areas.

Coloured pencils

The advantage of these is that they come in a huge variety of colours. Cartoons are usually drawn in a flat style, without much variation in light or shade, so you might need some practice in laying down areas smoothly.

Paper

A cheap sketch book is useful, because it lets you keep all of your drawings together. For special drawings, use high quality artists' paper with a smooth surface, which will not smudge as easily as rougher sketch paper.

Pencils need to be sharp to draw details, and blunter for filling in large areas.

Coloured pencils do not smudge like felt-tips.

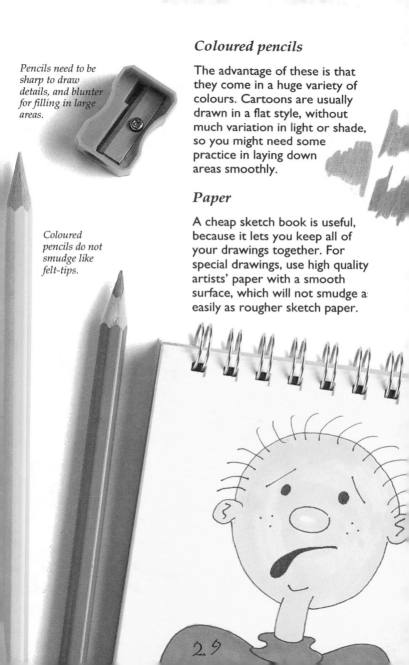

Mix and match

Here are lots of pictures of heads, bodies and legs from different sides. You can use them in your pictures. Remember that a person's head might be facing you while the body is sideways, and vice versa.

Happy

Laughing

Sad

Angry

Suspicious

Scared

Startled

Scheming

Happy

Laughing

Sad

Angry

Suspicious

Scared

Startled

Scheming

Long hair

Baseball cap

Braided hair

Woollen hat

Walking   Running   Waving   Hugging

Walking   Running   Arms folded   Pointing

Walking   Running   Standing   Dancing

Walking   Running   Jumping   Tiptoeing

Skinny legs   Short fat legs   Skidding   Climbing stairs

Index

This book is based on material previously published in *How to Draw Cartoons*.

ISBN 0-590-92185-1

Copyright © 1987, 1995 by Usborne Publishing Ltd.
All rights reserved. Published by Scholastic Inc., 555 Broadway, New York, NY 10012,
by arrangement with Usborne Publishing Ltd.

12 11 10 9 8 7 6 5 4 3 2 1   6 7 8 9/9 0 1/0
                                                                           08
Printed in the U.S.A.
First Scholastic printing, September 1996